FEMALE SINGERS
OF THE 1950's

PIANO / VOCAL / GUITAR

Catalog No. 44042
ISBN 978-1-922657-53-0

Produced by John L. Haag

Sales and Shipping:
Professional Music Institute LLC
1336 Cruzero Street, Box 128
Ojai, California 93024

Female Singers of the 1950's

PIANO / VOCAL / GUITAR

FEMALE SINGERS OF THE 1950'S

PIANO / VOCAL / GUITAR *continued*

Allegheny Moon

Lyric and Music by
Dick Manning and Al Hoffman

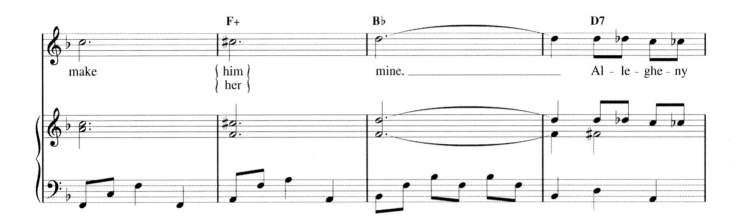

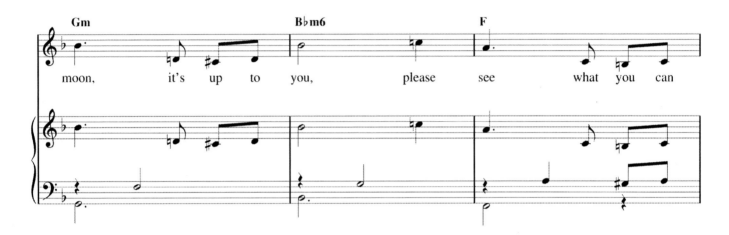

Botch - A - Me

(Ba-Ba-Baciami Piccina)

English lyric and music adapted by Eddie Y. Stanley
Italian lyric and music by R. Morbelli and L. Astore

Lyrics:

Botch-a-me, I'll botch-a-you and ev-'ry-thing goes cra-zy!

1. Bah, bah, botch-a-me, bam-bi-no, bah-bah bo, bo, bo-ca pic-co-li-no, when-a-you kiss me and I'm a-kiss-a you, tra-la-la-la-la-la-la-la-la

2.,3. Bah, bah, botch-a-me, my ba-by, bah-bah bo, bo, just say "yes" and may-be if-a-you squeeze me and I'm a-squeeze-a you, tra-la-la-la-la-la-la-la

8

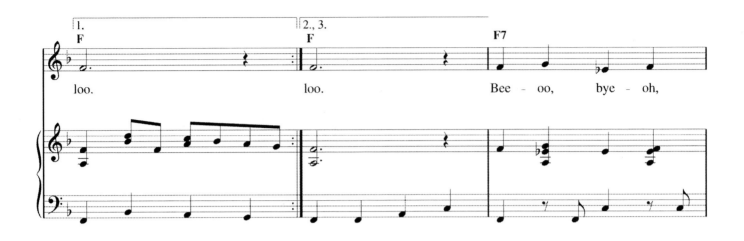

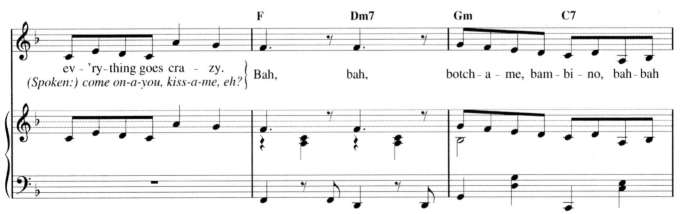

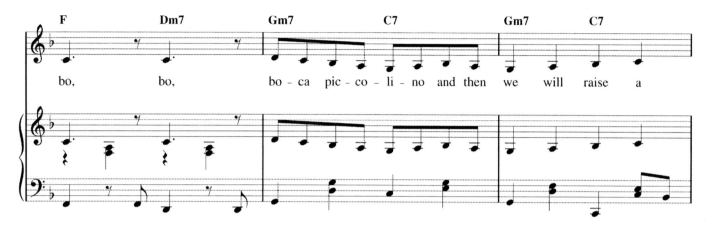

bo, bo, bo - ca pic - co - li - no and then we will raise a

To Coda *D.C al Coda*

great big fam - i - ly, tra - la - la - la - la - la - la - la lee.

Coda

tra - la - la - la - la - la - la - la, bee - oo, bye - oh, bee - oo boo,

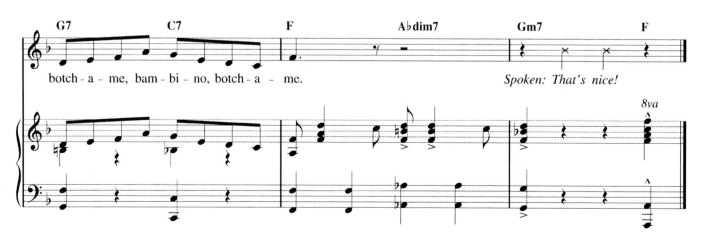

botch - a - me, bam - bi - no, botch - a - me. *Spoken: That's nice!*

Botch-a-me 3-3

Cross Over The Bridge

Lyric and Music by
George David Weiss and Bennie Benjamin

Moderately Slow with a Beat

1. If you're a guy who's had a gal in each and ev-'ry port, and
2. (If) you have built a boat to take you to the green-er side, and
3. (I) know it is-n't eas-y to re-sist temp-ta-tion's call, but

you for-got the rules of love that life has al-ways taught; and
if that boat is built of ev-'ry lie you ev-er lied, you'll
think of how your bro-ken heart will hurt you when you fall; 'cause

if you broke as man – y hearts as rip – ples in a stream, well,
nev – er reach the prom – ised land of love, I guar – an – tee; 'cause
some day you will find that you are hope – less – ly in love, and

broth – er, here's the on – ly way that you can be re – deemed!
lies can – not hold wa – ter, and you'll sink in – to the sea!
she'll be – long to some – one else as sure as stars a – bove!

Refrain

Cross o – ver tha bridge! Cross o – ver the bridge! Change your

12

Cross over the bridge 3-3

Dark Moon

Lyric and Music by
Ned Miller

Moderato (With a light beat)

Dark moon, _____ A-way up

high up in the sky, Oh tell me why, Oh tell me why you've lost your

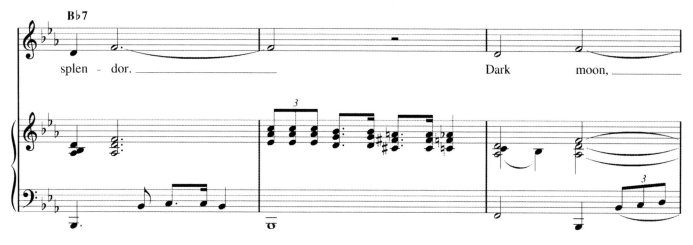

splen - dor. _____ Dark moon, _____

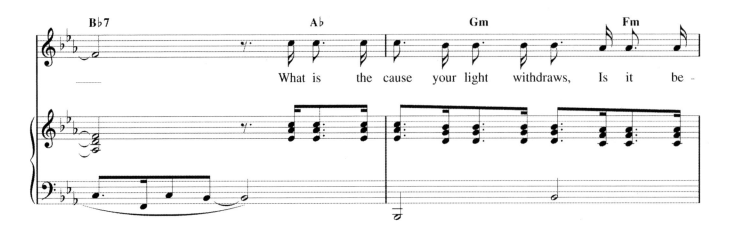

Dark moon 2-3

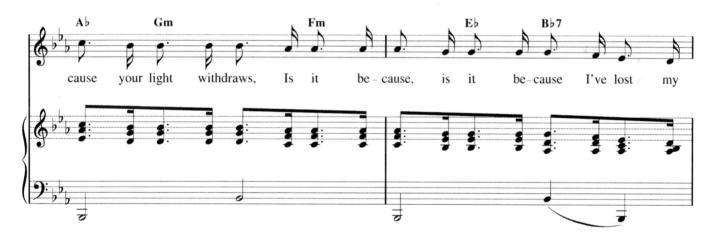

Dark moon 3-3

Diamonds Are A Girl's Best Friend

Lyric by Leo Robin
Music by Jule Styne

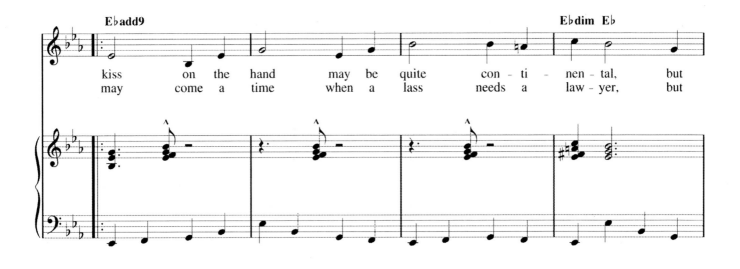

kiss on the hand may be quite con-ti-nen-tal, but
may come a time when a lass needs a law-yer, but

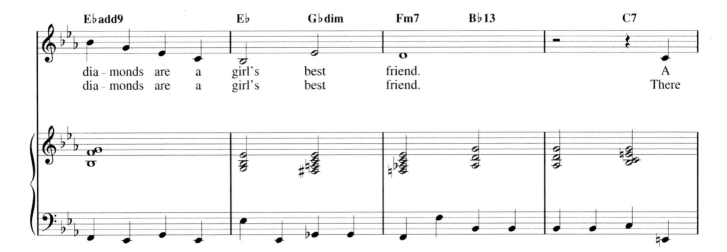

dia-monds are a girl's best friend.
dia-monds are a girl's best friend.
There

kiss may be grand but it won't pay the ren - tal on your
may come a time when a hard - boiled em - ploy - er thinks you're

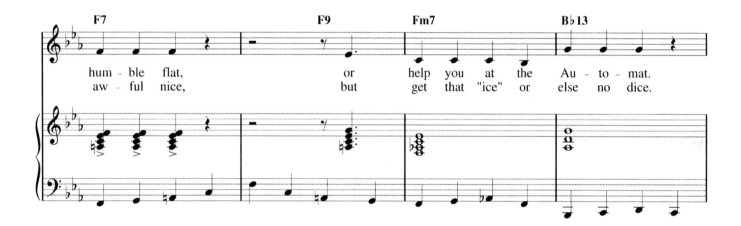

hum - ble flat, or help you at the Au - to - mat.
aw - ful nice, but get that "ice" or else no dice.

Men grow cold as girls grow old, and we
He's your guy when stocks are high, but be -

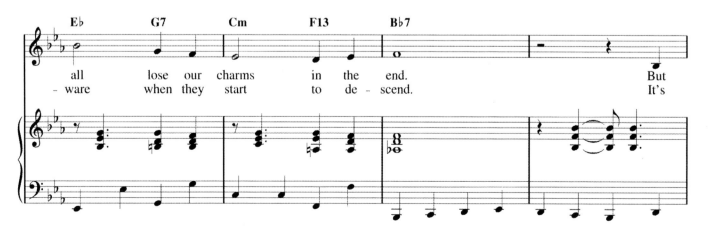

all lose our charms in the end. But
- ware when they start to de - scend. It's

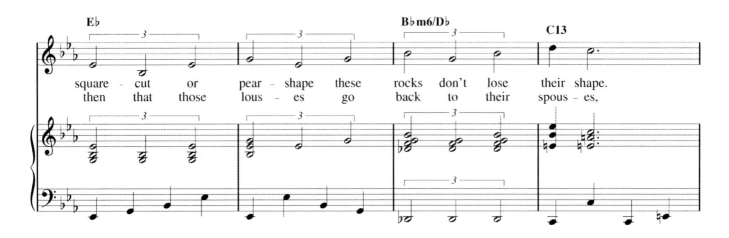

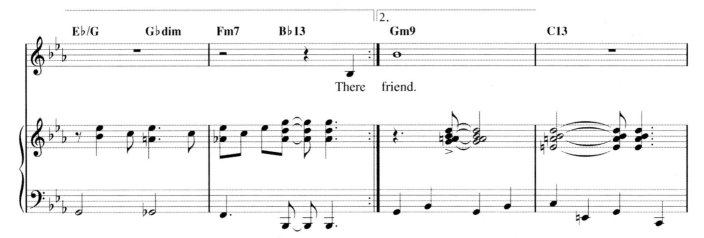

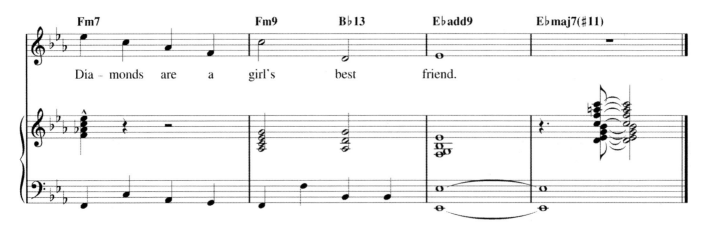

Diamonds are a girl's best friend 3-3

Everybody Loves A Lover

*Note: The 1st 16 bars of the Chorus and Refrain
may be sung and played simultaneously, as a duet.*

Lyric by Richard Adler
Music by Robert Allen

Moderato, with spirit

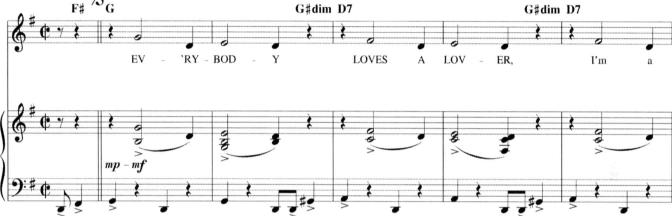

EV - 'RY - BOD - Y LOVES A LOV - ER, I'm a lov - er, Ev - 'ry - bod - y loves me. An - y - how, that's

how I feel, WOW! I feel just like a

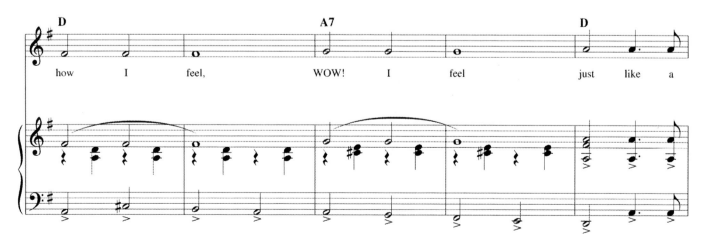

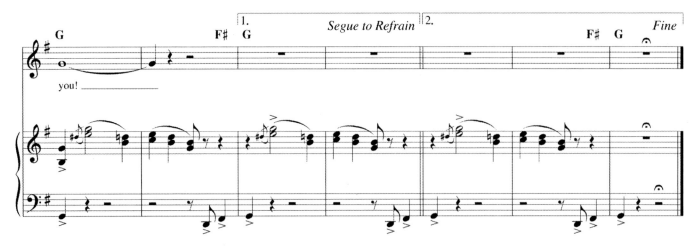

A Guy Is A Guy

Lyric and Music by
Oscar Brand

24

A guy is a guy 3-3

How Important Can It Be ?

Lyric and Music by
George David Weiss and Bennie Benjamin

Slowly and Expressively

How Much Is That Doggie In The Window ?

Lyric and Music by
Bob Merrill

30

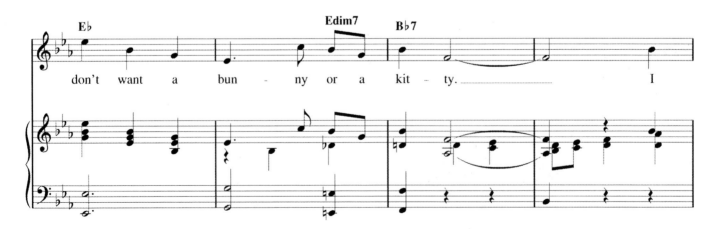

How much is that doggie in the window ? 3-5

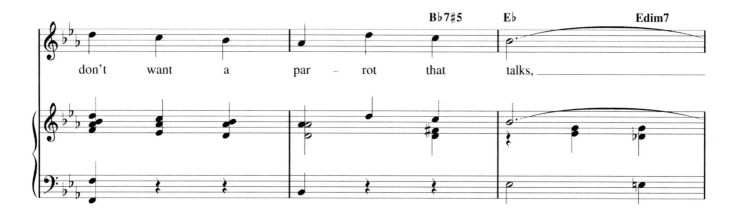

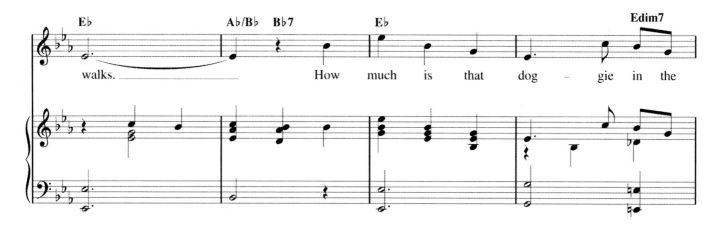

32

It's A Most Unusual Day

Lyric by Harold Adamson
Music by Jimmy McHugh

Moderately, not too slowly

Verse

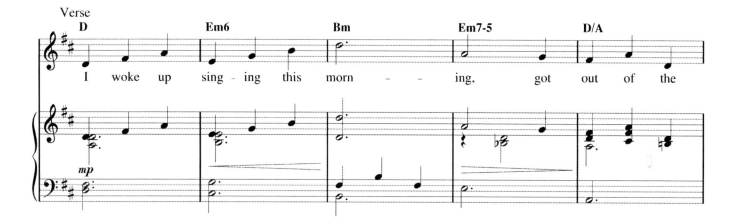

I woke up sing - ing this morn - - ing, got out of the

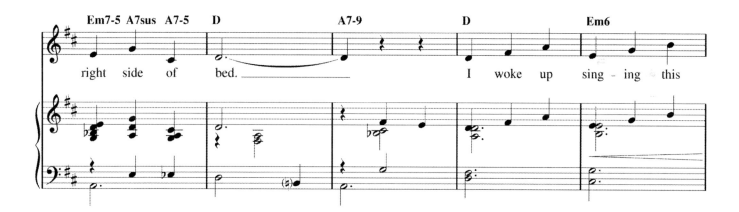

right side of bed. ____ I woke up sing - ing this

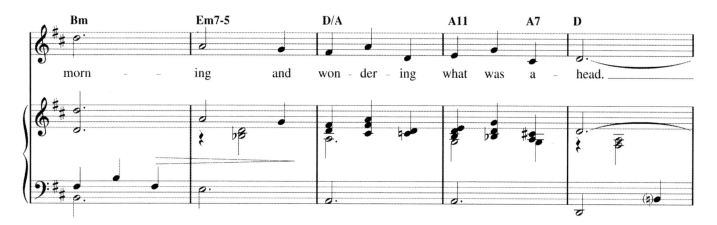

morn - - ing and won - der - ing what was a - head. ____

It's a most unusual day 3-5

It's So Nice To Have A Man Around The House

Lyric by Jack M. Elliot
Music by Harold Spina

3rd Chorus

It's so nice to have a man around the house,
Oh, so nice to have a man around the house,
Just a hero bold and vicious,
Who'll insist he get his wishes,
Oh, but first he'll do the dishes... It's so nice.
Oh, a house is just a house without a man,
He's the necessary evil in your plan;
Just a knight in shining armor,
Who is something of a charmer,
Though it's two to one you wind up with a louse,
It's so nice to have a man around the house.

4th Chorus

It's so nice to have a man around the house,
Oh, so nice to have a man around the house,
Just a guy who is attentive,
And who has a strong incentive,
To be more or less inventive...It's so nice.
Oh, a house is just a house without a man,
He's the necessary evil in your plan,
So put no one else above him,
When you love him really love him,
Even though he may be someone'else's spouse,
It's so nice to have a man around the house.

Make Yourself Comfortable

Lyric and Music by
Bob Merrill

Ooh, ooh, make your-self comf'-ta-ble; Ooh, ooh, make your-self comf'-ta-ble;

Ooh, ooh, make your-self comf'-ta-ble, ba - by. __

Ooh, ooh, make your-self comf'-ta-ble; Ooh, ooh,

I've got some rec-ords here To put you in the mood, The phone is off the hook So

Memories Of You

Lyric by Andy Razaf
Music by Eubie Blake

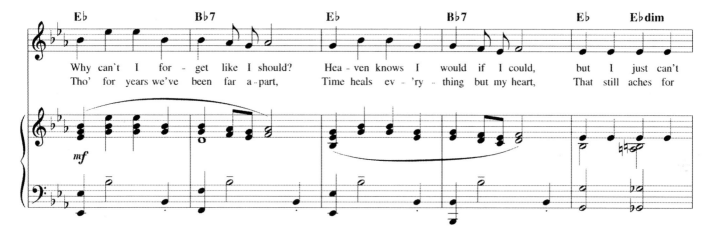

Why can't I for - get like I should? Hea - ven knows I would if I could, but I just can't
Tho' for years we've been far a - part, Time heals ev - 'ry - thing but my heart, That still aches for

keep you off my mind _____ Tho' you've gone, and love was in vain.
you the same old way _____ Seems I can't es - cape from the past.

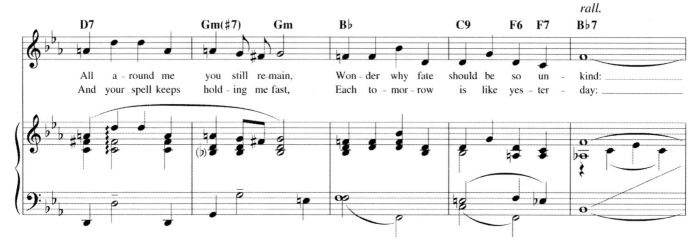

All a - round me you still re - main, Won - der why fate should be so un - kind: _____
And your spell keeps hold - ing me fast, Each to - mor - row is like yes - ter - day: _____

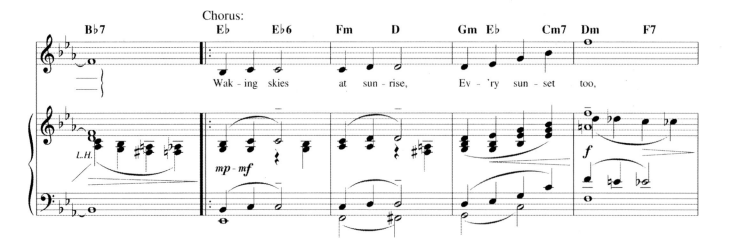

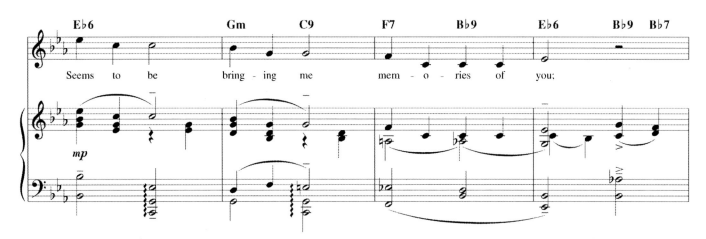

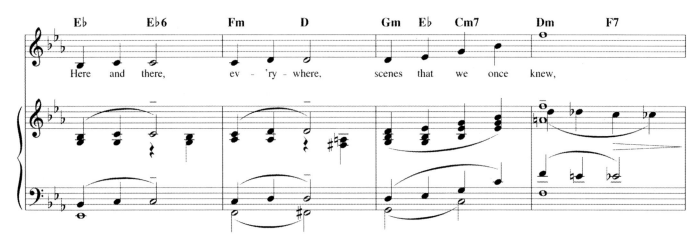

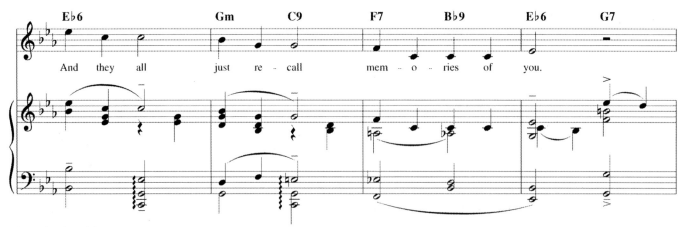

Mambo Italiano

Lyric and Music by
Bob Merrill

Freely

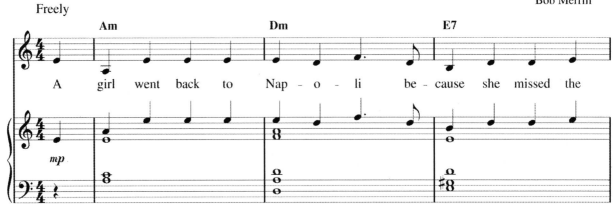

A girl went back to Nap - o - li be - cause she missed the

scen - er - y, the na - tive danc - es and the charm - ing songs. But wait a min - ute,

Medium Latin

something's wrong.

Hey mam - bo, mam - bo I - tal - i - an - o
Instrumental

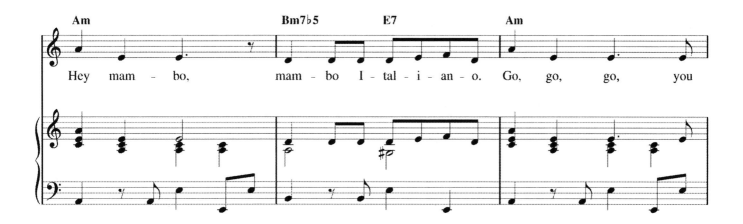

Hey mam - bo, mam - bo I - tal - i - an - o. Go, go, go, you

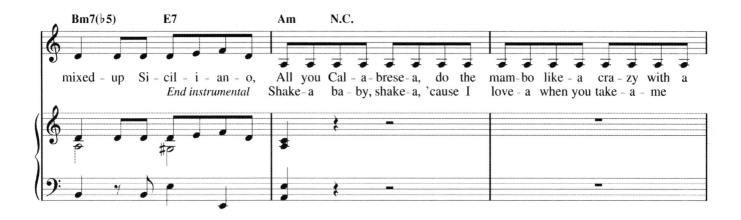

mixed - up Si - cil - i - an - o, All you Cal - a - brese - a, do the mam - bo like - a cra - zy with a

End instrumental Shake - a ba - by, shake - a, 'cause I love - a when you take - a - me

Hey mam - bo, don't wan - na tar - an - tel - la. Hey mam - bo,

Instrumental

no more the moz - za - rel - la. Hey mam - bo, mam - bo I - tal - i - an - o.

End Instrumental

48

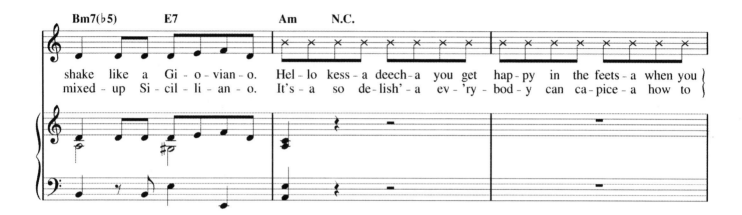

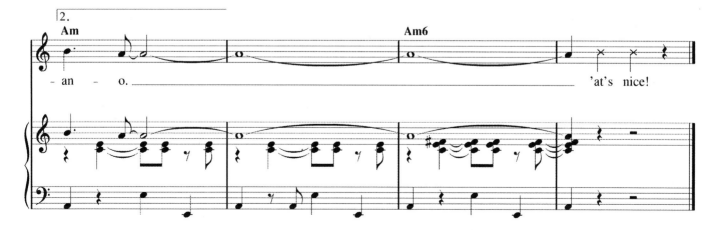

Mambo italiano 4-4

May You Always

Lyric and Music by
Larry Marks and Dick Charles

May you al-ways walk in sun-shine, slum-ber warm when night winds blow. May you al-ways

live with laugh-ter for a smile be-comes you so. May good for-tune find your door-way,

may the blue-bird sing your song. May no trou-ble trav-el your way, may no wor-ry stay too long.

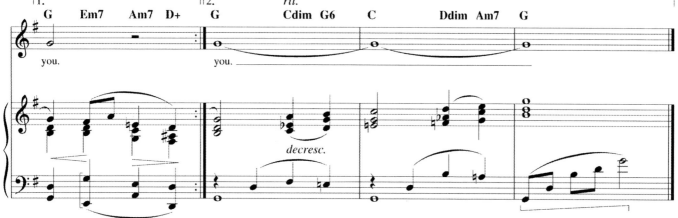

Mockin' Bird Hill

Lyric and Music by
Vaughan Horton

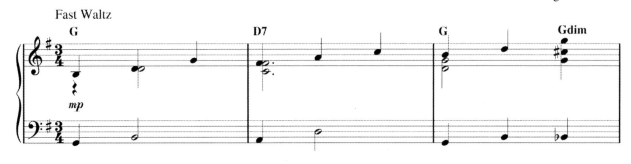

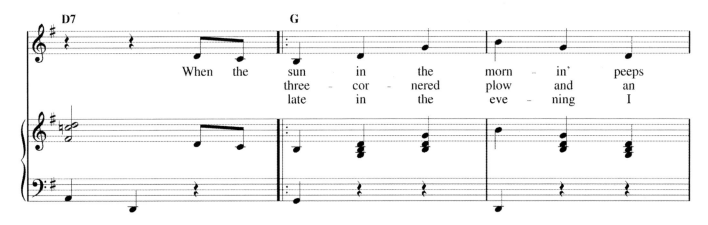

When the sun in the morn — in' peeps
three — cor — nered plow and an
late in the eve — ning I

o — ver the hill and kiss — es the
a — cre to till and a mule that I
climb up the hill and sur — vey all my

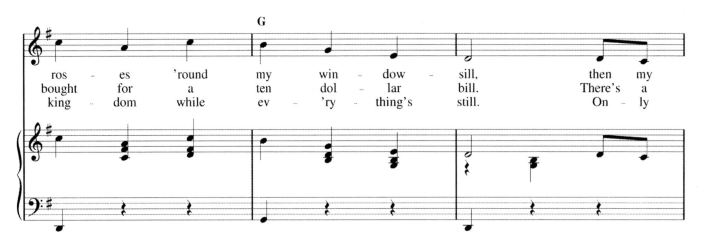

ros — es 'round my win — dow — sill, then my
bought for a ten dol — lar bill. There's a
king — dom while ev — 'ry — thing's still. On — ly

53

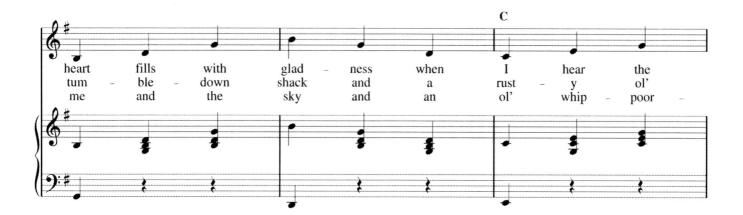

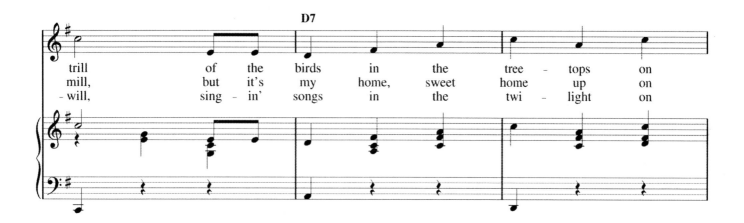

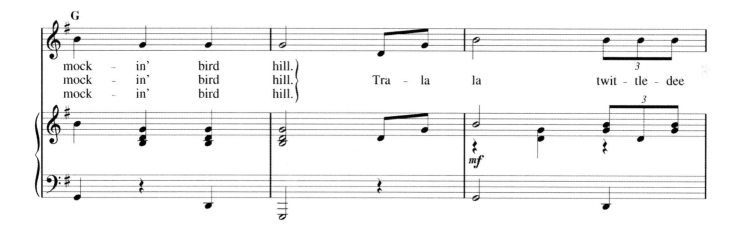

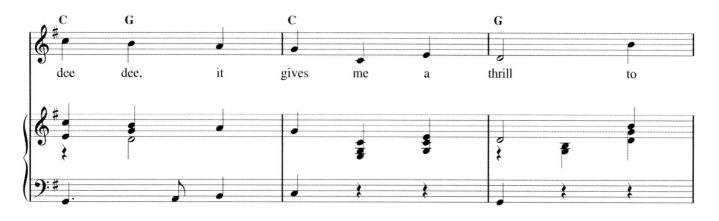

Mockin' bird hill 2-3

54

Mockin' bird hill 3-3

Mr. Wonderful

(From The Musical "Mr. Wonderful")

Lyric and Music by
George David Weiss, Jerry Bock and Larry Holofcener

56

I must tell you what my heart knows is true:

Mis - ter Won - der - ful, _____ that's you!

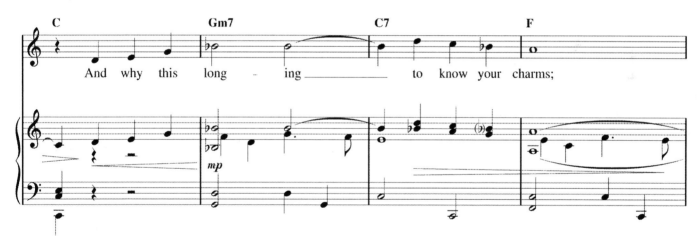

And why this long - ing _____ to know your charms;

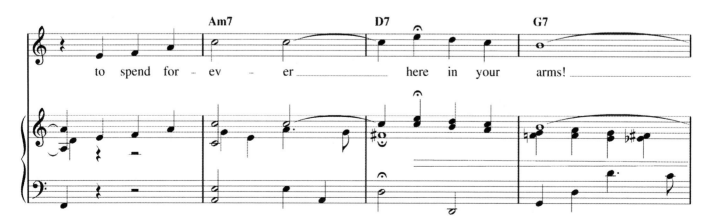

to spend for - ev - er _____ here in your arms! _____

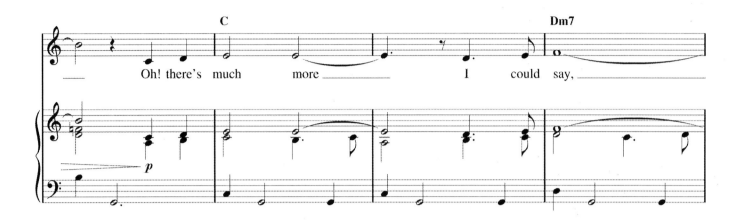

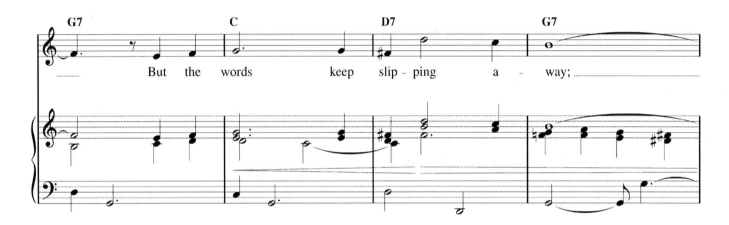

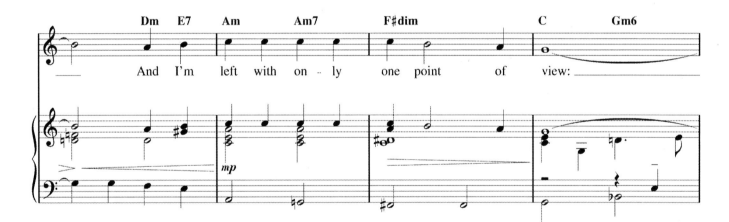

59

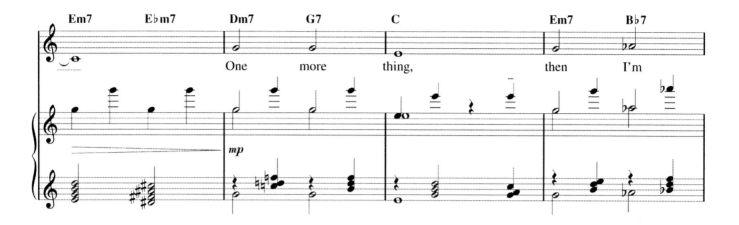

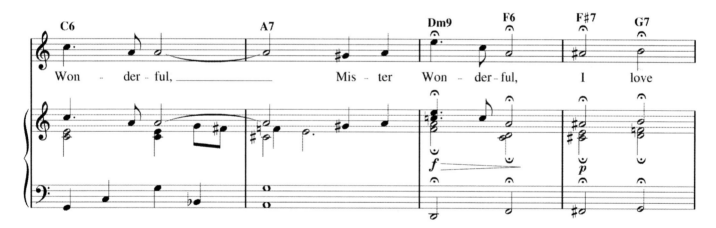

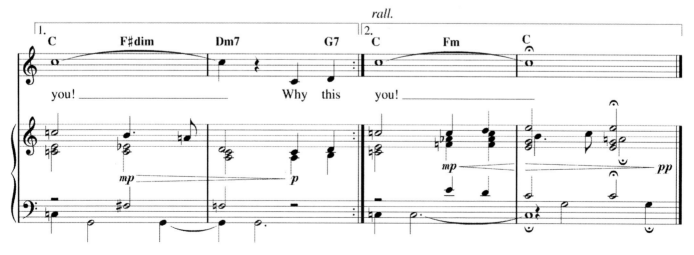

Mr. Wonderful 5-5

Music! Music! Music!

(Put Another Nickel In)

Lyric and Music by
Stephan Weiss and Bernie Baum

I'd do an - y - thing for you. ___ An - y - thing you'd want me to. ___

G7 **G7-5** **C7** **F**

All I want is kiss-ing you ___ and Mu - sic! Mu - sic! Mus - sic!

C7 **F**

Clos - er, ___ my dear, come clos - er. ___ The ni - cest

part of an-y mel-o-dy_____ is when you're danc-ing close to me,_____ So,

put an-oth-er nick-el in, ___ in the nick-el -o-de -on ___

All I want is loving you_ and Mu - sic! Mu-sic! Mu - sic! Mu - sic!

Ricochet Romance

Lyric and Music by
Norman Gimbel, Larry Coleman and Joe Darion

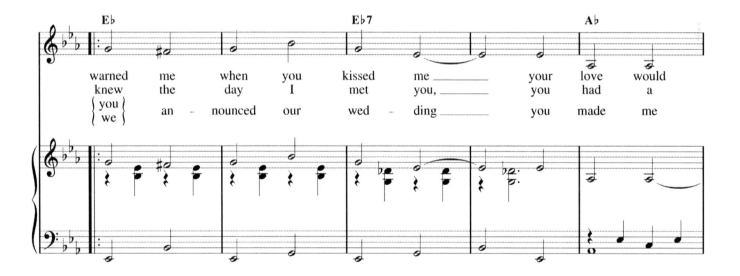

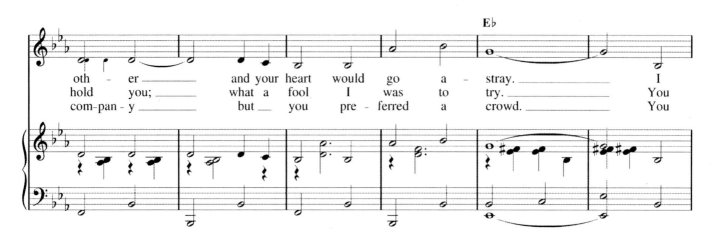

oth - er _____ and your heart would go a - stray. _____ I
hold you; _____ what a fool I was to try. _____ You
com-pan - y _____ but you pre - ferred a crowd. _____ You

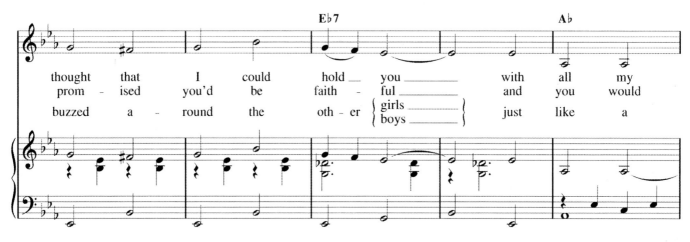

thought that I could hold _ you _____ with all my
prom - ised you'd be faith - ful _____ and you would
buzzed a - round the oth - er { girls _____ } just like a
                                   { boys _____ }

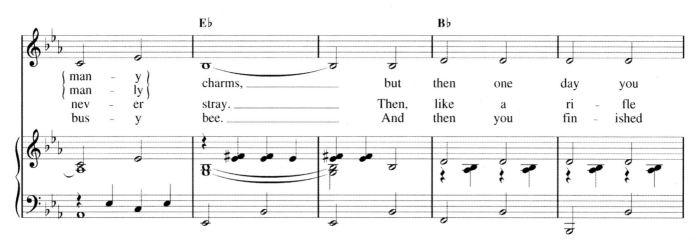

{ man - y }   charms, _____ but then one day you
{ man - ly }
nev - er   stray. _____ Then, like a ri - fle
bus - y   bee. _____ And then you fin - ished

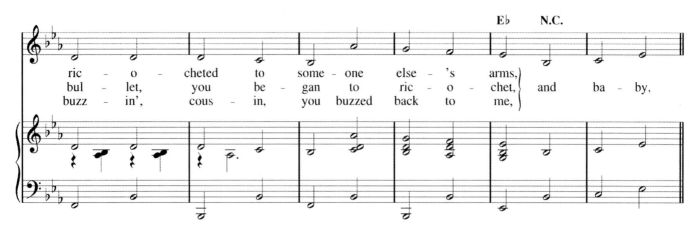

ric - o - cheted to some - one else - 's arms, }
bul - let, you be - gan to ric - o - chet, } and ba - by,
buzz - in', cous - in, you buzzed back to me, }

My Happiness

Lyric by Betty Peterson
Music by Borney Bergantine

Slowly, with expression

Eve-ning sha-dows make me

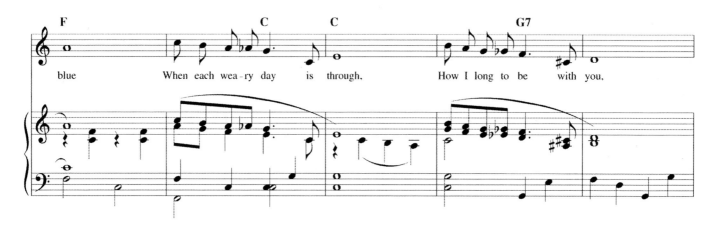

blue When each wea-ry day is through, How I long to be with you,

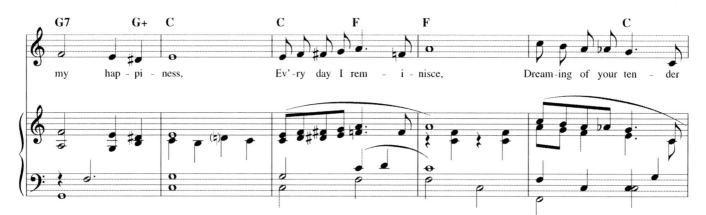

my hap-pi-ness, Ev'-ry day I rem - i - nisce, Dream-ing of your ten - der

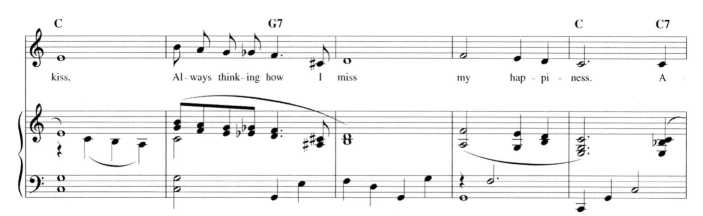

kiss, Al-ways think-ing how I miss my hap-pi - ness. A

mil - lion   years it seems   Have gone by   since   we shared our dreams,   But I'll

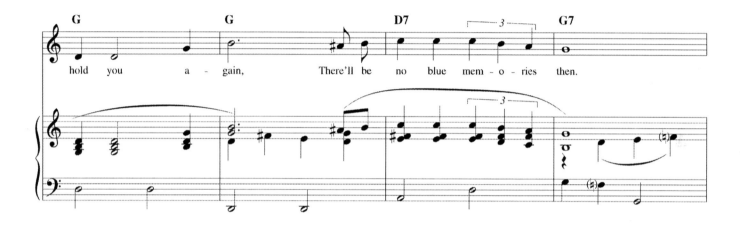

hold   you   a - gain,   There'll be   no   blue mem - o - ries   then.

Wheth - er skies are gray   or   blue,   An - y place on earth   will   do,

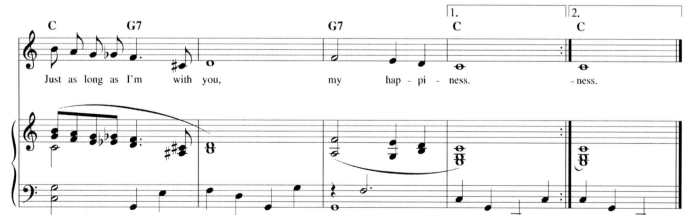

Just as long as I'm   with you,   my   hap - pi - ness.   - ness.

My happiness 2-2

My Heart Cries For You

Lyric by Carl Sigman
Music by Percy Faith

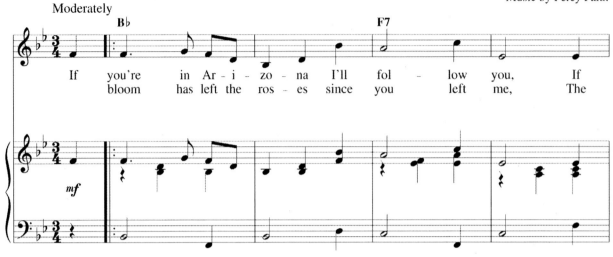

If you're in Ar - i - zo - na I'll fol - low you, If
bloom has left the ros - es since you left me, The

you're in Min - ne - so - ta I'll be there too. You'll have a mil - lion
birds have left my win - dow since you left me. I'm lone - ly as a

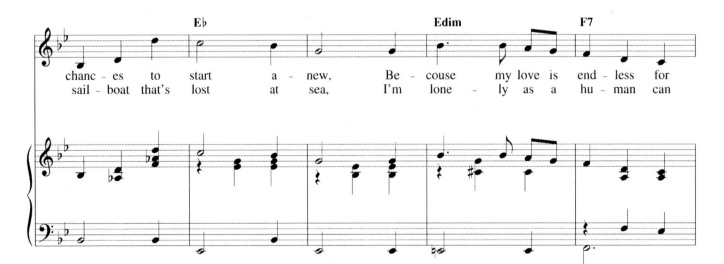

chanc - es to start a - new, Be - couse my love is end - less for
sail - boat that's lost at sea, I'm lone - ly as a hu - man can

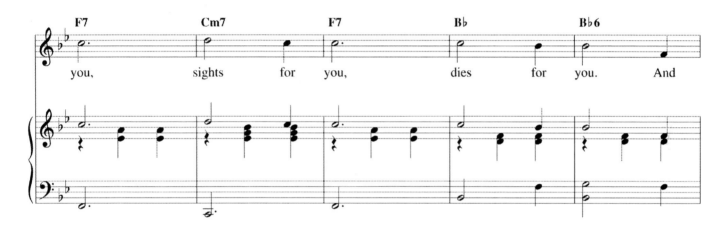

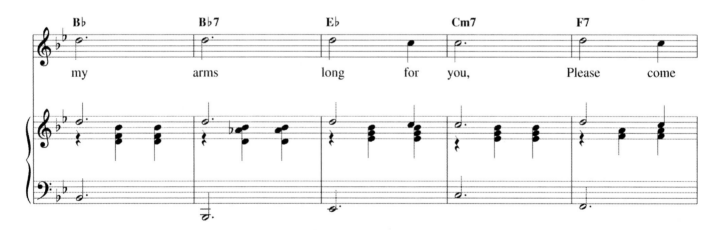

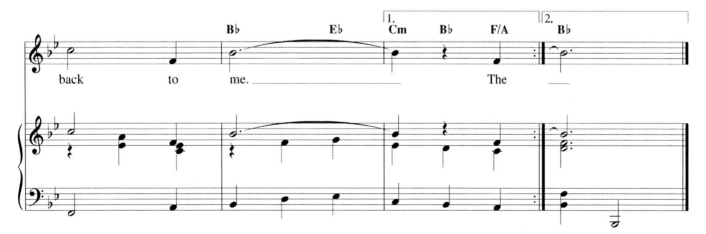

My heart cries for you 2-2

Pledging My Love

Lyric and Music by
Ferdinand "Fats" Washington and Don Robey

For-ev-er, my Dar-ling, _____ Our love will be true, _____ Always and for-

-ev-er, _____ I'll love just_ you. _____ Just promise me, Dar-ling, _____ your love in re-

-turn. _____ Make this fire in my soul, dear, _____ for-ev-er burn. My

hearts at your command. Dear, to keep, love, and to hold. Mak-ing you

hap-py's my de-sire,___ Dear,___ keep-ing you is my goal. I'll for-ev-er

love you,___ the rest of my days. I'll nev-er part

from you___ and your lov-ing ways.___ For-ev-er, my ways.___

Sentimental Journey

Lyric and Music by
Bud Green, Les Brown and Ben Homer

74

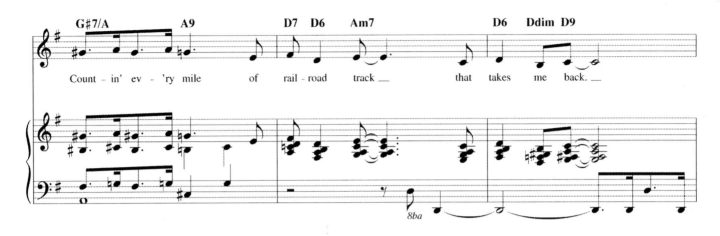

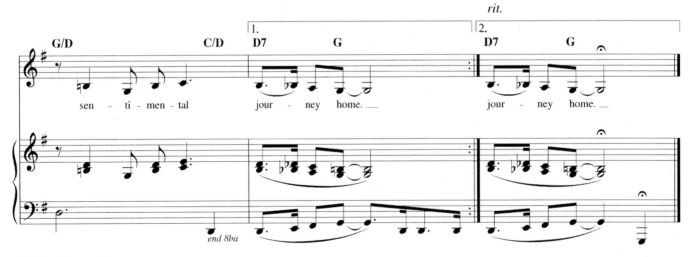

Sentimental journey 3-3

Teach Me Tonight

Lyric by Sammy Cahn
Music by Gene DePaul

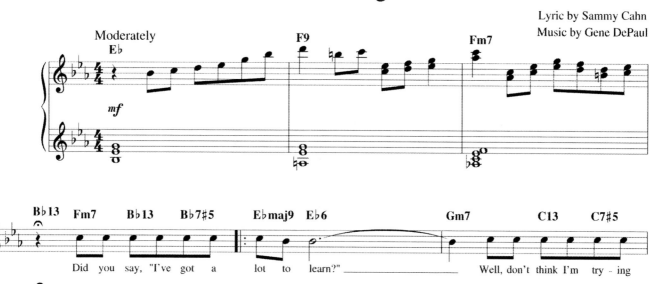

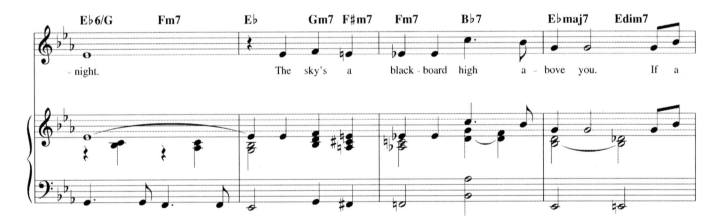

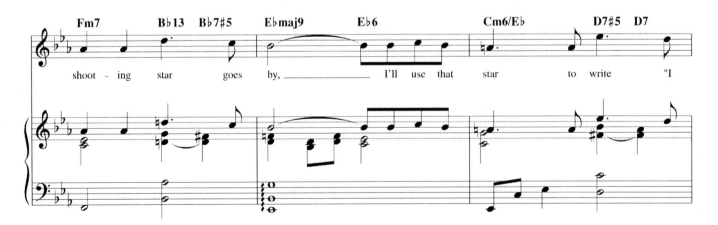

Teach me tonight 2-3

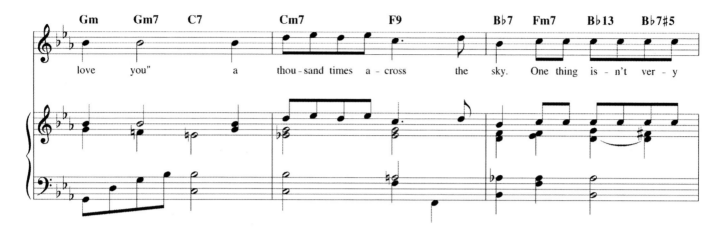

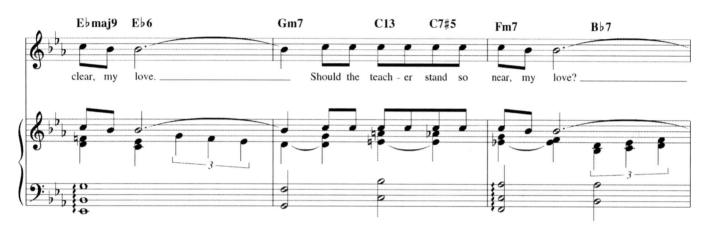

A Sweet Old Fashioned Girl

Lyric and Music by
Bob Merrill

80

There Goes My Heart

Lyric by Benny Davis
Music by Abner Silver

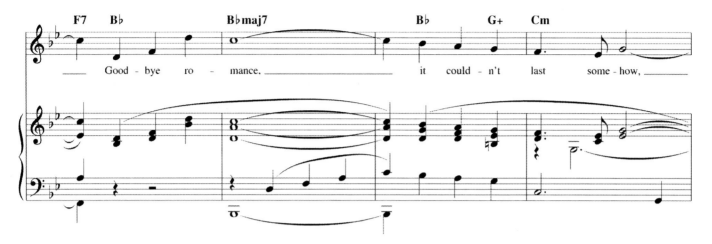

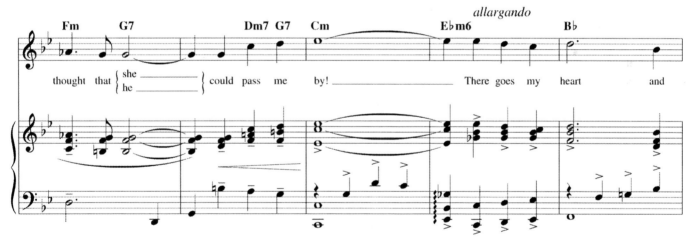

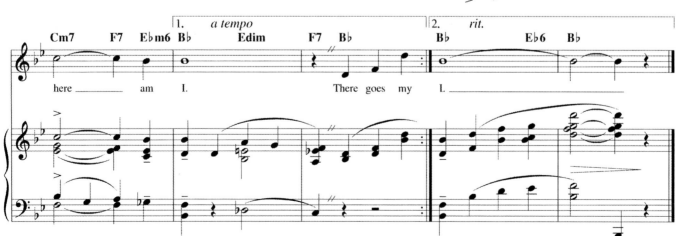

There goes my heart 2-2

This Ole House

Lyric and Music by
Stuart Hamblen

Country 2-beat

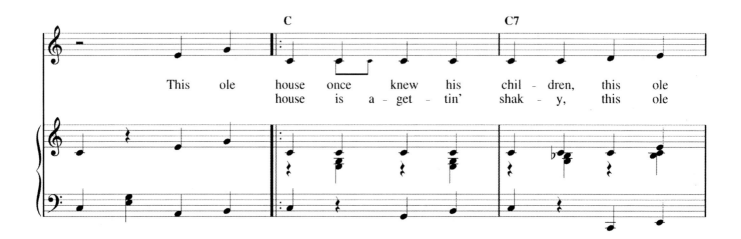

This ole house once knew his chil - dren, this ole
house is a - get - tin' shak - y, this ole

house once knew his wife, this ole house was home and
house is a - get - tin' old, this ole house lets in the

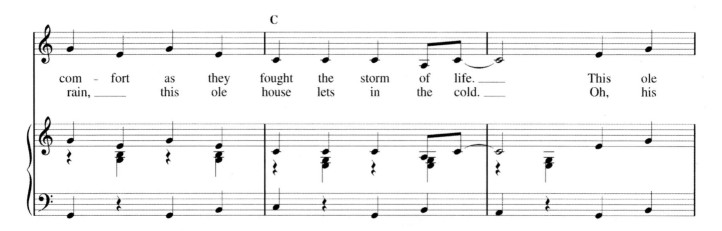

com - fort as they fought the storm of life. ___ This ole
rain, ___ this ole house lets in the cold. ___ Oh, his

This ole house 2-6

This ole saints.

End instrumental This ole

house is a - fraid of thun - der, this ole house is a - fraid of

This ole house 4-6

storms, this ole house just groans and trem-bles when the night wind flings its

arms. This ole house is a-get-tin' fee-ble, this ole house is-a need-in'

paint, just like him it's tuck-ered out but he's a-get-tin' read-y to meet the

saints. Ain' a-gon-na need this house no long-er, ain' a-gon-na need this house no

This ole house 5-6

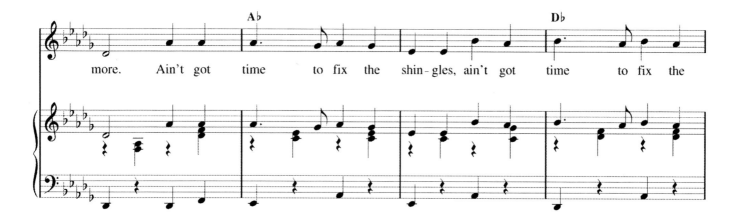

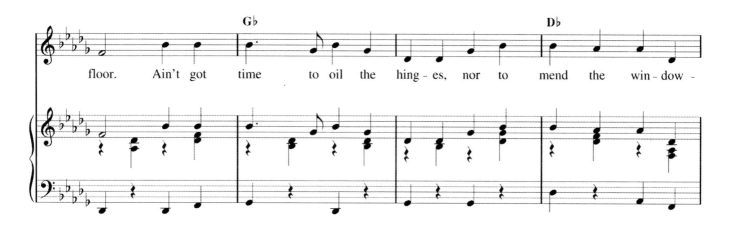

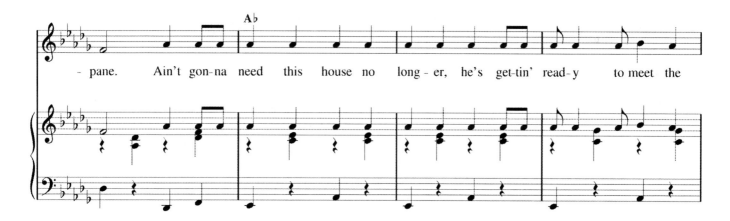

This ole house 6-6

Too Young To Go Steady

Lyric by Harold Adamson
Music by Jimmy McHugh

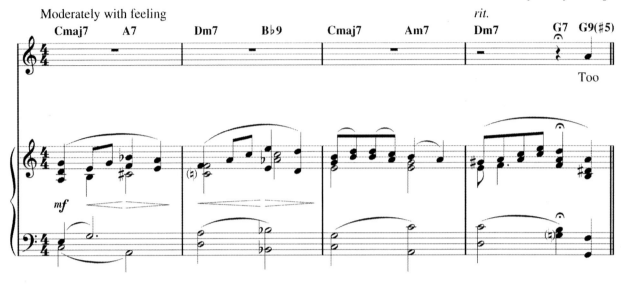

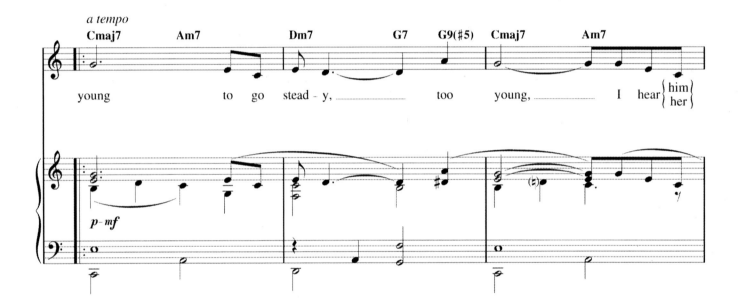

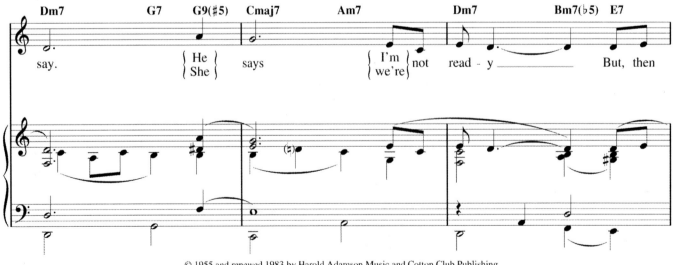

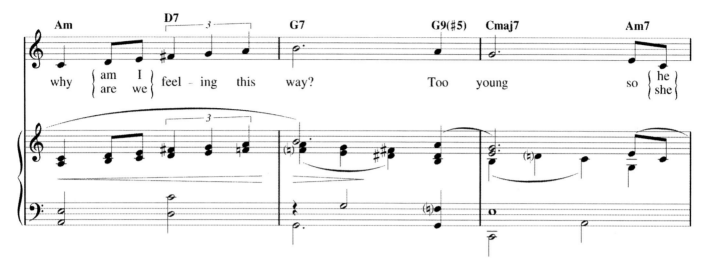

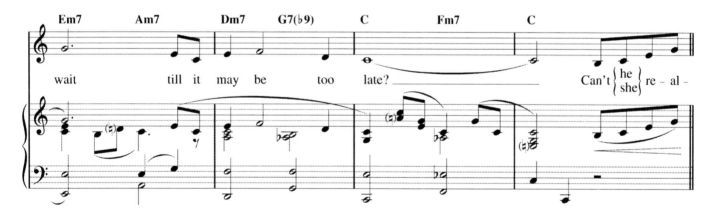

Too young to go steady 2-3

92

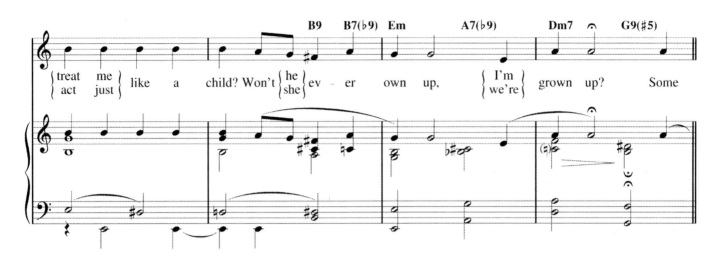

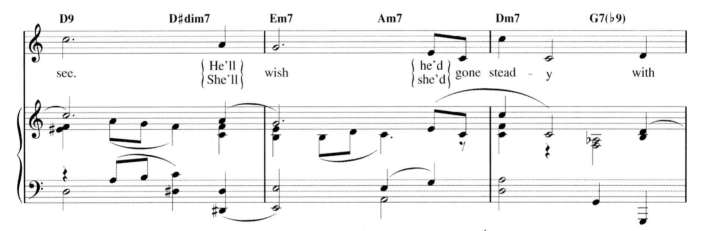

Vaya Con Dios
(May God Be With You)

Lyric and Music by
Larry Russell, Inez James and Buddy Pepper

Moderate waltz tempo

Now the

ha - ci - en - da's dark _____ the town is sleep - ing _____ Now the time has come to part, _____

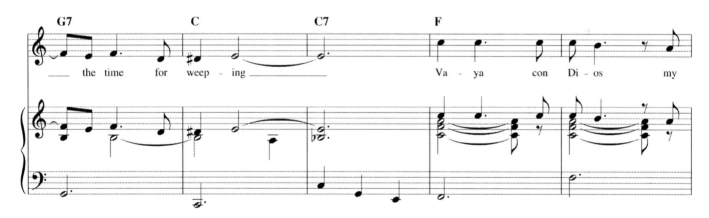

_____ the time for weep - ing _____ Va - ya con Di - os my

dar - ling, _____ May God be with you my love. _____

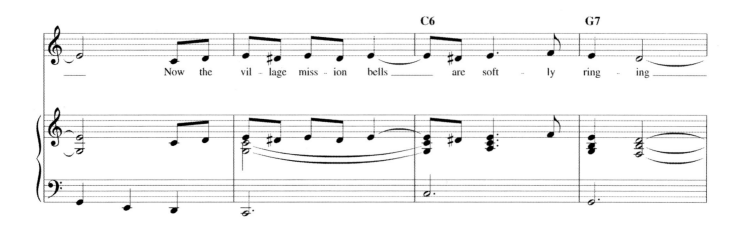

Now the vil - lage miss - ion bells ____ are soft - ly ring - ing ____

If you list - en with your heart ____ you'll hear them sing - ing ____

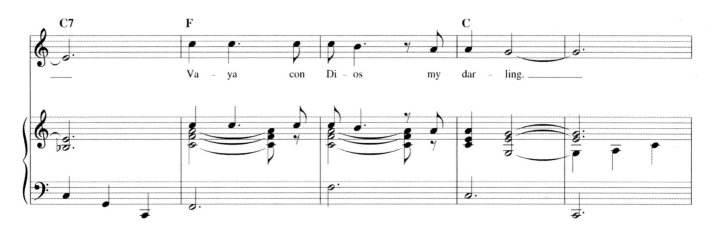

Va - ya con Di - os my dar - ling. ____

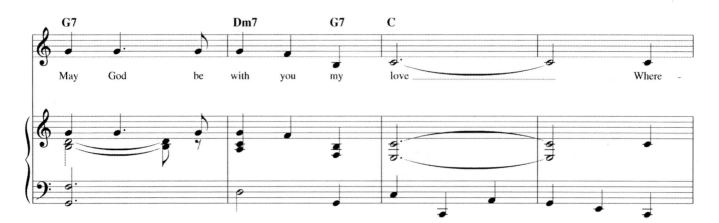

May God be with you my love ____ Where -

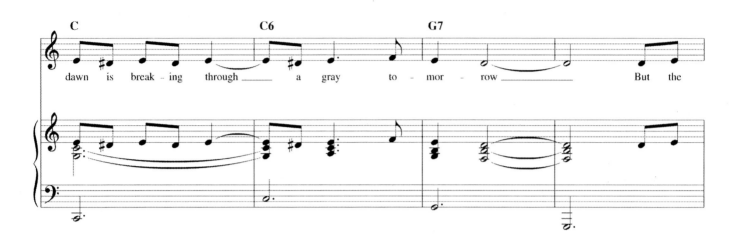

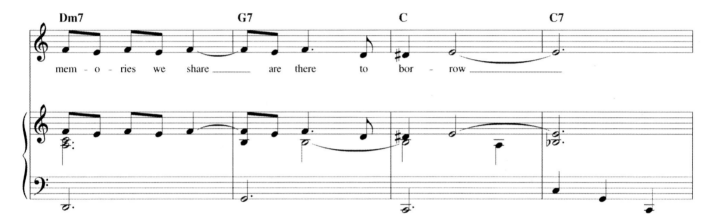

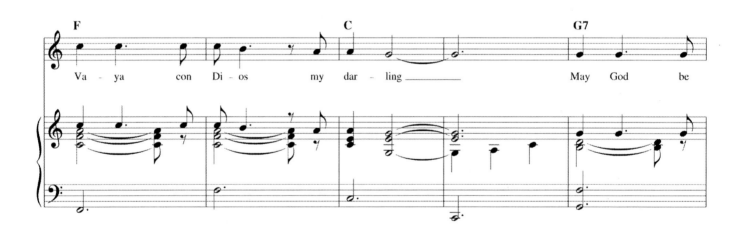

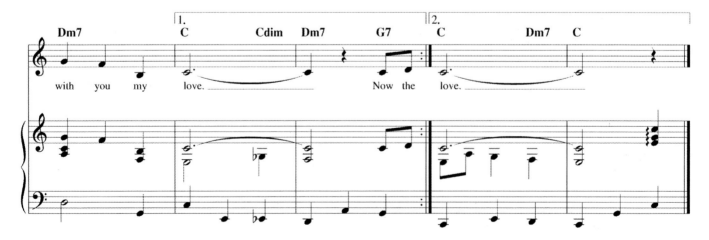

Vaya Con Dios

Lyric and Music by
Larry Russell, Inez James and Buddy Pepper

Vaya con Dios mi vida
Vaya con Dios mi amor

Se llegó ya el momento de separarnos
En silencio el corazón dice y suspira

Vaya con Dios mi vida
Vaya con Dios mi amor

Las campanas de la iglesia suenan tristes
Y parece que al sonar también te dicen

Vaya con Dios mi vida
Vaya con Dios mi amor

Adonde vayas tu, yo iré contigo
En sueños siempre junto a ti estaré
Mi voz escucharás, dulce amor mío
Pensando como yo estarás
Volvernos siempre a ver

La alborada al despertar feliz te espera
Si en tu corazón yo voy a donde quiera

Vaya con Dios mi vida
Vaya con Dios mi amor
Vaya con Dios mi vida
Vaya con Dios mi amor

What A Diff'rence A Day Made

(Cuando Vuelva A Tu Lado)

Lyric by Stanley Adams
Music by Maria Grever

What a diff-'rence a day made, _____ Twen-ty four lit-tle ho - - urs, _____
Cuan-do vuel-va a tu la - do, _____ No me nie-gues tus be - - sos, _____

Brought the sun and the flow - ers, _____ Where there used to be rain. _____
Que el a-mor que te he da - do, _____ No po-drás ol-vi - dar. _____

My yes-ter-day was blue dear, _____ To - day I'm part of
No me pre-gun-tes na - da, _____ Que na - da he de ex-pli-

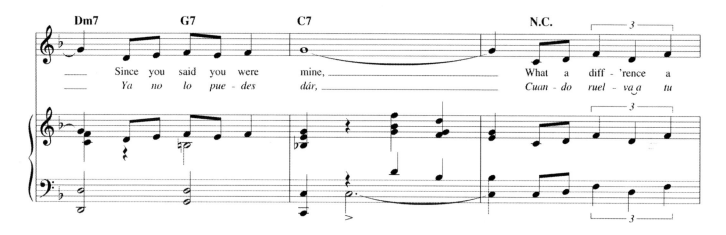

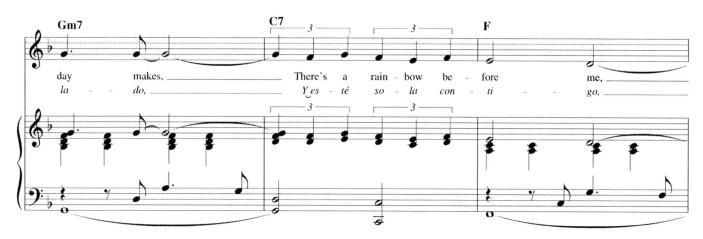

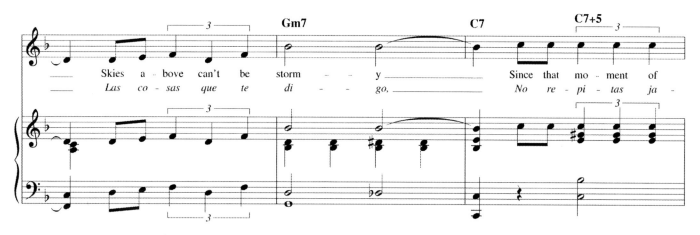

What a diff'rence a day made 2-3

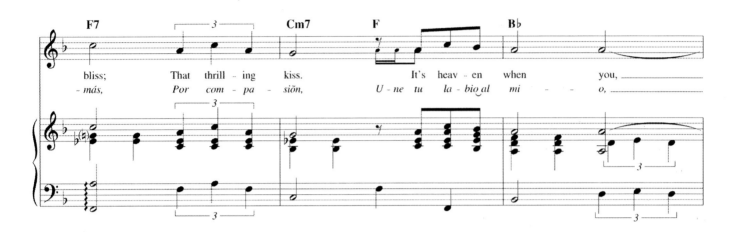

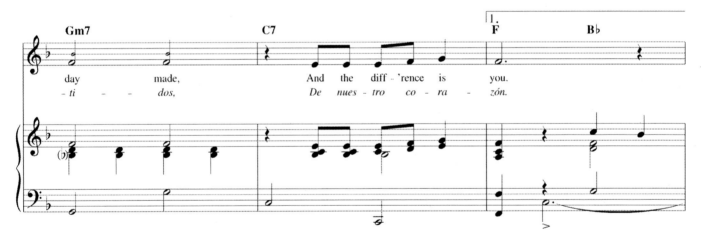

What a diff'rence a day made 3-3

Why Don't You Believe Me ?

Lyric and Music by Lew Douglas,
Luther King Laney and Leroy W. Rodde

102

Who's Sorry Now ?

Lyric by Harry Ruby and Bert Kalmar
Music by Ted Snyder

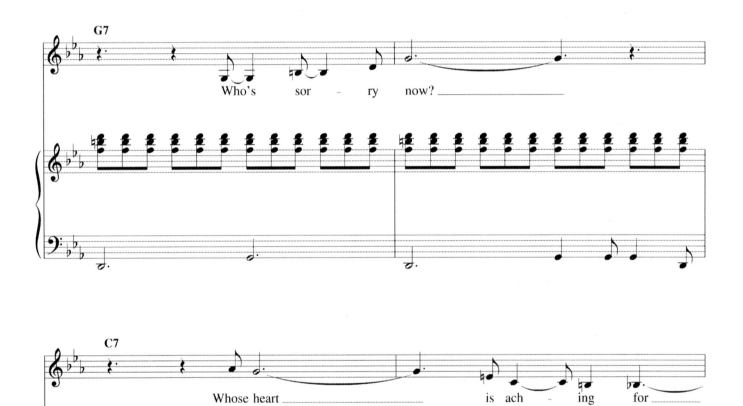

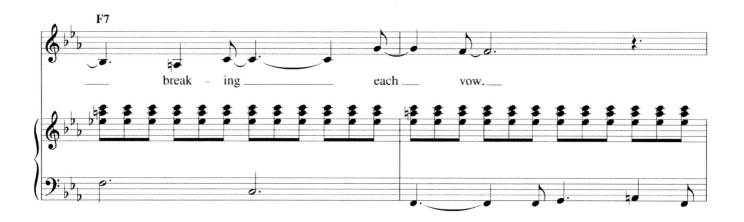

F7

break - ing ____ each ___ vow. ___

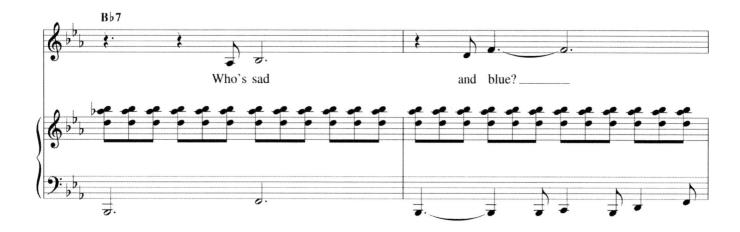

Bb7

Who's sad   and blue? _____

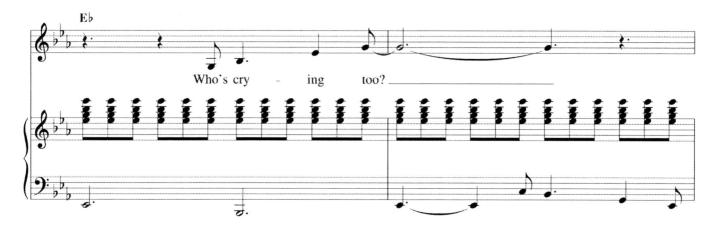

Eb

Who's cry - ing too? _____

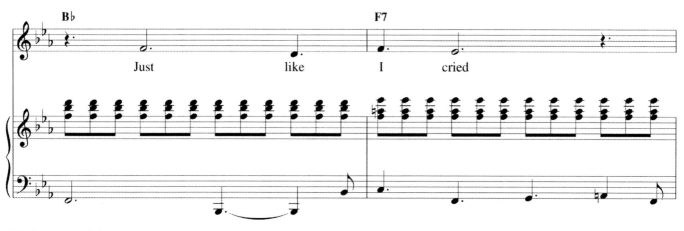

Bb   F7

Just   like   I   cried

Who's sorry now ? 2-6

106

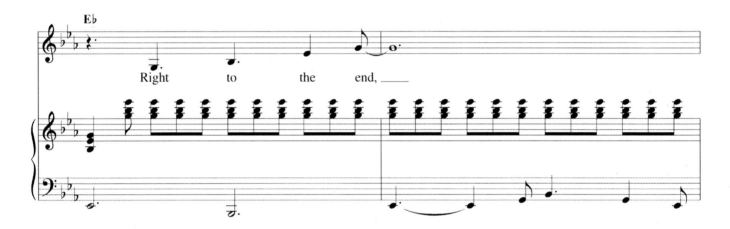

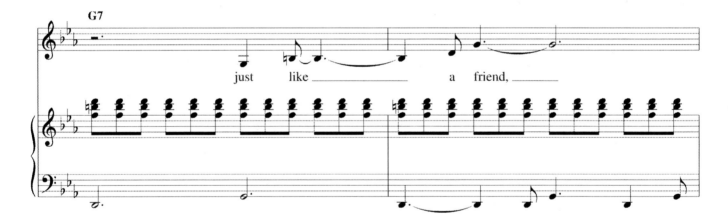

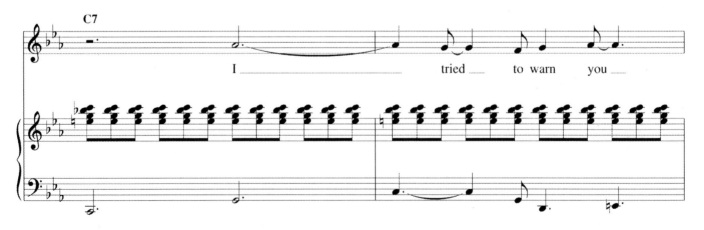

Who's sorry now ? 3-6

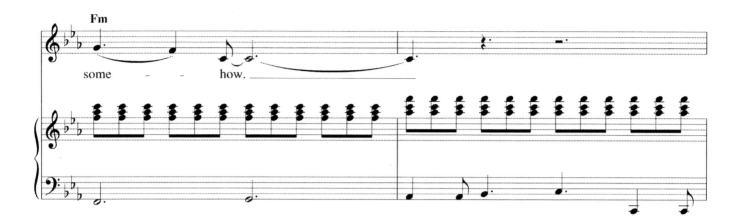

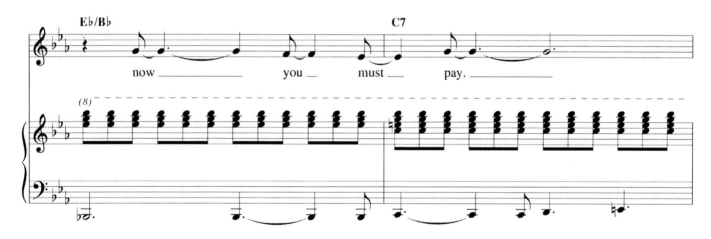

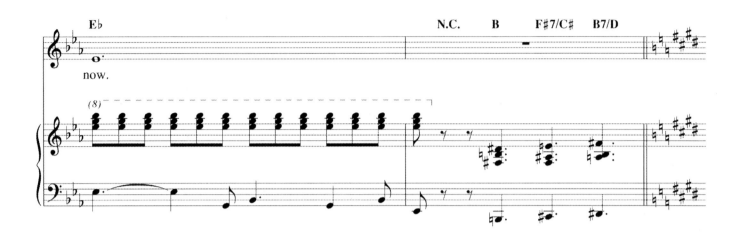

now.

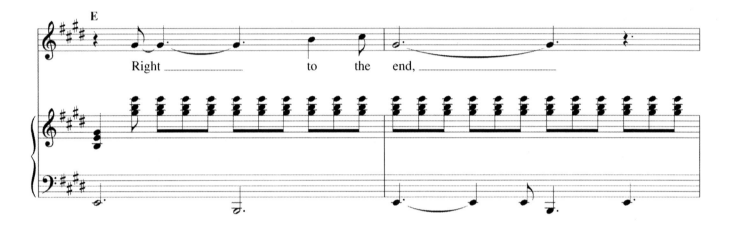

Right _____ to the end, _____

just _____ like ___ a friend. _____

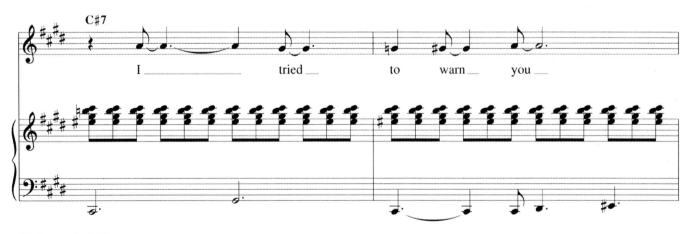

I _____ tried ___ to warn ___ you ___

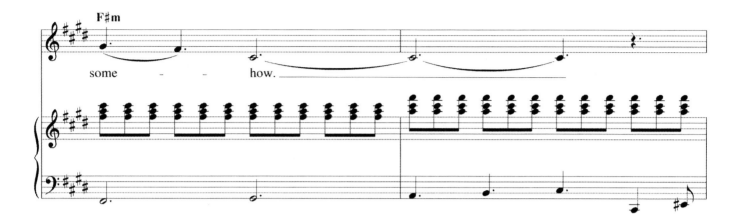

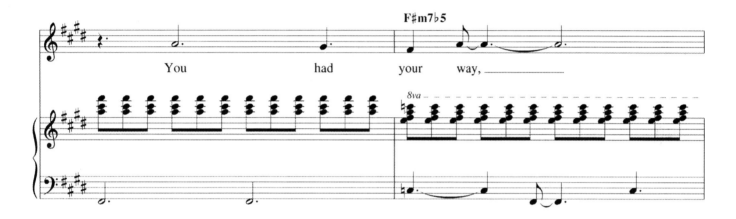

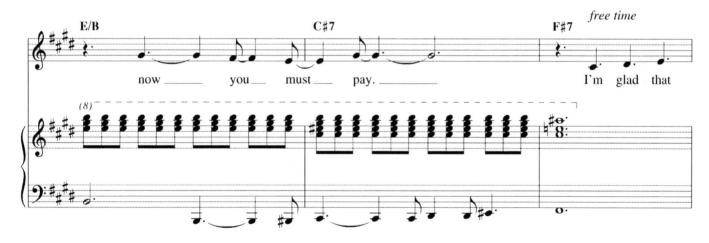

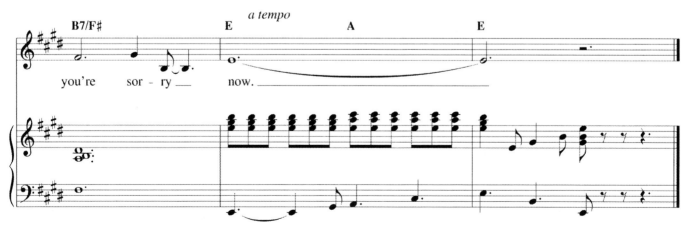

Who's sorry now ? 6-6

Wheel Of Fortune

Lyric and Music by
George David Weiss and Bennie Benjamin

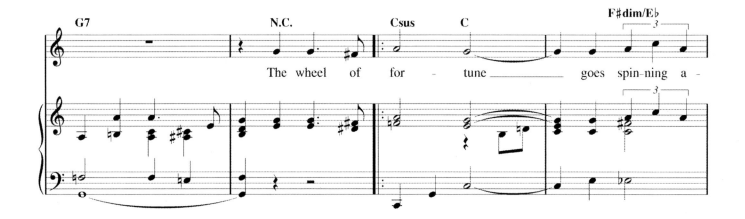

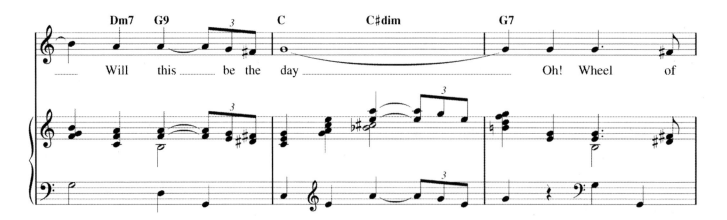

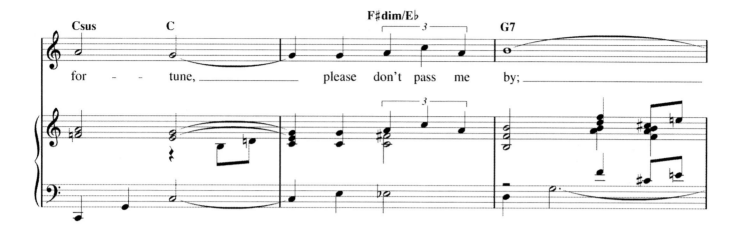

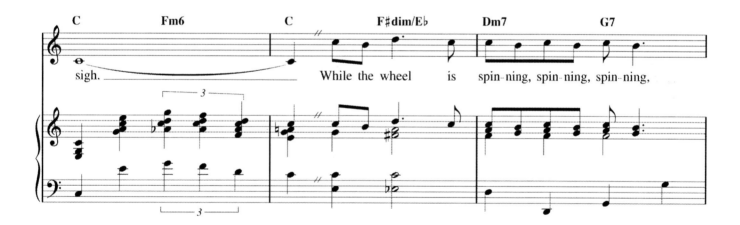

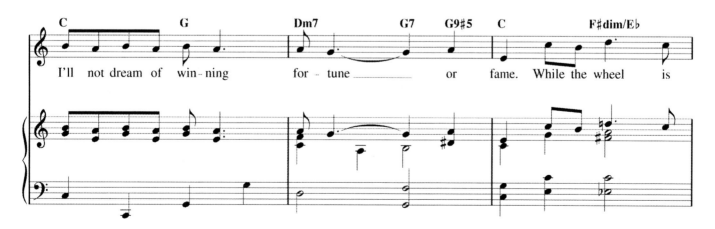

Wheel of fortune 2-3

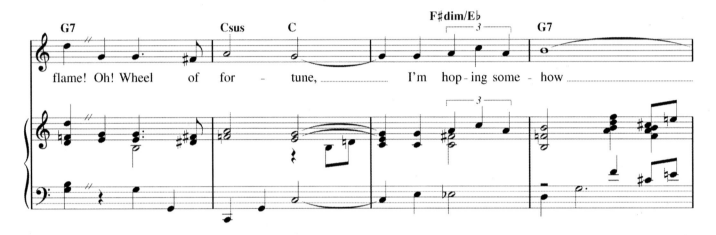